Contents

BIRMINGHAM CITY UNIVERSITY
Book no. 34530703
Subject 220 Kna
LIBRARY

Mary Jones' Bible........................... 4

What is in the Christian Bible?...... 6

The books of the Bible 8

The Old Testament Bible Story 10

The New Testament Bible Story 12

The history of the Bible 14

Using the Bible 18

Using the Bible for song 20

The Ten Commandments.............. 22

Poetry in the Bible.......................... 24

Parables in the Bible...................... 26

Psalms in the Bible........................ 28

Letters in the Bible......................... 30

Index... 32

(Title page) A copy of the New International Version of the Holy Bible. *(Right)* A boy studying from a children's Bible.

The fish shown on the cover is an ancient symbol of Christianity. The letters of the Greek word for fish (ichthus), are the first letters of each word in the sentence, "Jesus Christ of God, the Son, the Saviour". Also, Jesus often called the Apostles "fishers of men".

Mary Jones' Bible

Mary wanted a Bible of her own – even if it took her six years hard work and a barefoot walk of 45 kilometres!

The word Bible means simply, 'the books', in Greek. The Bible is the word of God handed down to us.

The Bible has many stories in it, and we shall look at some later in this book. But we will begin with a story of a girl who really wanted to own her own Bible. She was called Mary Jones.

▲ Mary Jones saved to buy a Bible in the Welsh language, like this one.

Mary Jones' story

Mary Jones was born on December 16, 1784, into a poor Welsh family. Each week the family walked to church to listen to stories from the Bible. Mary wanted to learn more, but her family was too poor to own a Bible. Instead, she had to use the Bible belonging to a neighbour.

How was Mary to get a Bible of her own? She would need to earn money.

Mary's neighbour helped by giving her some chickens so that she could sell their eggs. It did not bring in much money, but Mary saved every little bit she earned.

Mary tried other ways of getting money, too. She looked after other children, she knitted socks and, in fact, she did more or less anything she could just to save up money for her Bible.

It took six years of hard work before Mary had enough money. She was just 15 years old.

The nearest place she could get a Bible was from a preacher 45 kilometres away. That was two days' walk. Mary walked all that way barefoot so that she would not wear out her precious shoes.

When she got to the preacher's house she was told that all of the Bibles had already been promised to other people. Mary sobbed and told her story to the preacher.

The preacher took pity on Mary and made her take the last Bible, saying that the person it had been promised to could wait a little longer.

Mary's efforts encouraged some people to start up a society for giving Bibles to the poor.

What happened to Mary's Bible? It was given to a library where it remains safe to this day, over two hundred years later.

Weblink: www.CurriculumVisions.com

While Jesus was still speaking, someone came from the house of Jairus, the synagogue ruler. "Your daughter is dead," he said. "Don't bother the teacher any more." Hearing this, Jesus said to Jairus, "Don't be afraid; just believe, and she will be healed – he took her by the hand and said, "My child, get up!" Her spirit returned, and at once she stood up.

▲ Stories like this one inspired Mary Jones to want her own copy of the Bible.

▶ This girl is reading a modern Welsh Bible like the one that Mary Jones worked so hard to buy. Today, there are many organisations that translate the Bible into other languages and give copies away.

What is in the Christian Bible?

The Christian Bible contains many books, some written long before the birth of Jesus Christ, and some after.

The Bible is the most widely read book ever and sixty million new copies are printed each year.

The Bible is actually made up of many smaller books. The first book in the Bible is called Genesis, and the last book is called Revelation. The books in the Bible were written by many different people over nearly 1,500 years.

The parts of the Bible

The first part of the Bible talks about events before the birth of **JESUS CHRIST**. This is called the **OLD TESTAMENT**. There are 39 books common to all versions of the Old Testament.

▲ It takes about 75 hours to read the Bible aloud at a normal rate. Fifty hours of that will be spent reading the Old Testament and 25 hours reading the New Testament.

The second, and shorter, part tells about events after the birth of Jesus Christ. This is called the **NEW TESTAMENT**. There are 27 books common to all versions of the New Testament.

Old Testament

This is also called the Jewish, or Hebrew, Bible because most of the books in it are also shared with Jewish people and it was written in **HEBREW**, the language of the Jewish people.

The first five books were given by God to Moses. They tell the story of the Jewish people from the creation of the Earth to the death of Moses. Some of the things in the Old Testament that you may be familiar with are the story of the Garden of Eden and the Ten **COMMANDMENTS**.

New Testament

This is all about the life of Jesus Christ and the founding of the Christian **CHURCH**. The New Testament contains the four **GOSPELS** (Matthew, Mark, Luke and John), a section on history called the Acts of the Apostles, and a section called **EPISTLES**, which contains letters written to early Christian churches by **APOSTLES**. It finishes with the Book of Revelation.

Many Bibles

The Bible was originally written in ancient forms of Hebrew and Greek. But there have been many translations of the Bible into almost all of the languages of the world. The most famous English translation is the King James version. It was first produced in 1611.

Some people feel that the way things are written in this Bible makes it hard to read, although others think it is very beautifully written.

There are many other, newer Bibles now, including some on the Internet and some written in very modern English.

Apocrypha

The **PROTESTANT** Bible consists of 66 books. The **ROMAN CATHOLIC** and Eastern **ORTHODOX** Bibles include other books, called **APOCRYPHA**, not recognised by Protestant Christians. The Apocrypha are books of religious materials that the Jewish people did not accept as **SCRIPTURE** but which appeared in the Greek and Latin translations of the Old Testament. Most of the Apocrypha tell about the time in Jewish history when **ISRAEL** was conquered by the Babylonian and Greek empires and many Jews were taken as captives to Babylon (in modern day Persia and Iraq).

◀▼ This priest is reading a Greek Orthodox Bible. The Greek Orthodox Bible is written in Greek and contains some extra books and Psalms that are not in the Protestant version of the Bible.

The books of the Bible

The Bible is made up of many smaller books. Each book tells many stories.

Welcome to the Bible

The Bible is one of the most exciting books ever written. It has the most dramatic beginning it is ever possible to have – the story of how the universe, the Earth and everything on it was created by God.

The Bible also contains plenty of scary stories, wars, narrow escapes, tales of life and death, stories about ordinary people, slaves and kings.

The Christian Bible also has a very dramatic ending – the killing of its main character, Jesus, and then his **RESURRECTION** from the dead.

Some of the people in the stories are not always good, and some of them are very bad.

Every story in the Bible helps us to understand God and how to live according to God's wishes. Many of the stories in the Bible can also help us to learn other things, such as how to get along with other people.

Even though the Bible tells us about events that happened thousands of years ago in a far-off land, we can see that these stories still have meaning to us today.

The order of stories in the Bible

The Bible is made up of many separate books. Each book is made up of chapters and verses and in modern copies of the Bible each chapter and verse is numbered. This makes it easy to find passages and to tell what part you are reading.

▼▶ These are the books in the Protestant Bible. They are usually divided up into sections, based on what is in each book.

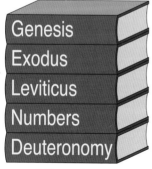

Genesis
Exodus
Leviticus
Numbers
Deuteronomy

The Law
(The five books of Moses)

Joshua
Judges
Ruth
1 Samuel
2 Samuel
1 Kings
2 Kings
1 Chronicles
2 Chronicles
Ezra
Nehemiah
Esther

Historical books

Job
Psalms
Proverbs
Ecclesiastes
Song of Songs

Wisdom books

Isaiah
Jeremiah
Lamentations
Ezekiel
Daniel

Major prophets

Weblink: www.CurriculumVisions.com

For example, Genesis 1:2 is the second verse of the first chapter of the book of Genesis:

> *Now the Earth was formless and empty, darkness was over the surface of the deep, and the Spirit of God was hovering over the waters. (Genesis 1:2)*

The stories in the Bible do not always happen in order, so you have to skip around a bit in order to read things that happened in order. For example, the dedication of the Temple of King Solomon is told of in 1 Kings, but stories about the rest of King Solomon's reign are told in a later book, 2 Chronicles.

In order to read the Bible, it helps if you are familiar with some of the things that happen in each book. So, on the following pages you will find some short descriptions of the books of the Bible.

Minor prophets
Hosea
Joel
Amos
Obadiah
Jonah
Micah
Nahum
Habakkuk
Zephaniah
Haggai
Zechariah
Malachi

Minor prophets

Gospels and Acts
Matthew
Mark
Luke
John
Acts

Gospels and Acts

Paul's Epistles
Romans
1 Corinthians
2 Corinthians
Galatians
Ephesians
Philippians
Colossians
1 Thessalonians
2 Thessalonians
1 Timothy
2 Timothy
Titus
Philemon

Paul's Epistles (letters)

Other Epistles
Hebrews
James
1 Peter
2 Peter
1 John
2 John
3 John
Jude

Other Epistles (letters)

Prophecy
Revelation

Prophecy

The Old Testament Bible Story

In the Old Testament you can find stories about the first people on Earth, how people began worshipping God, and the story of ancient Israel.

▲ God's creation of Adam. Michelangelo's painting on the ceiling of the Sistine Chapel, the Vatican, Rome.

The first five books

Genesis: The book of Genesis starts with the beginning of creation and the story of Adam and Eve, the beginnings of the different nations and of civilization. In this book you can find the stories of Cain and Abel, of Noah and the flood, of Sodom and Gomorrah, and of the Tower of Babel. It ends with the story of Abraham (also called Abram) and his family and God's promise to Abraham to make him the father of a great nation if he accepts God's laws.

Genesis 12: Abraham is called by God

The LORD had said to Abram, "Leave your country, your people and your father's household and go to the land I will show you.

I will make you into a great nation and I will bless you."
(Genesis 12:1–2)

Exodus: The book of Exodus tells about how God brought the Jewish people out of slavery in Egypt. This book is where you can find the story of Moses and the Ten Commandments, and the story of the Golden Calf. In this book God hands down laws for worship and for living according to God's wishes.

> **Exodus 20: Giving of the Ten Commandments**
>
> *And God spoke all these words: "I am the LORD your God, who brought you out of Egypt, out of the land of slavery."*
> *(Exodus 20:1–2)*

Leviticus: This book describes how the priestly tribe, the Levites, are supposed to perform all the worship rituals, including how to build an altar, how to atone (make good) for committing sin, how to make **SACRIFICES**, and the rules for how priests and ordinary people should worship. It also describes what should be done on the Sabbath.

Numbers: This book tells the story of how the Jewish people wandered in the desert for 40 years before finding the **PROMISED LAND** and of how they conquered the people living there and established the nation of Israel.

Deuteronomy: This book contains the messages of Moses during the last years of his life. As his followers prepare to cross the Jordan River and enter the Promised Land, Moses retells the story of how they fled from Egypt and reminds people of God's laws.

The historical books

The next 12 books are called the historical books because they tell stories about the history of ancient Israel. In these books you can find stories about King David, King Solomon, Samson, Goliath, Ahab and many others.

Wisdom writings

These five books (Job, Psalms, Proverbs, Ecclesiastes and the Song of Songs) talk about important questions of life and faith.

The book of Job tries to answer the question, "Why do people suffer?" Psalms contains poems, hymns and songs praising and worshipping God. Proverbs and Ecclesiastes contain advice and sayings that help teach people how to live a good life. The Song of Songs (also called the Song of Solomon) is a poem about love which teaches that love is a gift from God.

Prophets

The next 17 books were each written by a different **PROPHET**. A prophet is a person who has a special relationship with God and who may receive messages from God.

Many of the books of the prophets tell about things that will happen in the future, including the coming of the **MESSIAH**, whom Christians believe was Jesus. These books also stress the need for people to **REPENT**, and of God's love for the people.

The New Testament Bible Story

The New Testament books tell the story of Jesus Christ and the beginning of the Christian faith.

The New Testament contains 27 books in four parts: the four Gospels, Acts, the Epistles (or letters) and Revelation.

The Gospels

The word 'gospel' means 'good news', and these four books tell the good news that God has provided salvation through the life, death and resurrection of Jesus. So, they can be thought of as stories about the life of Jesus Christ.

They were written by four early Christians and followers of Jesus – Matthew, Mark, Luke and John. Even though all four Gospels tell

Matthew 1: Jesus is born

…an angel of the Lord appeared to him in a dream and said, "Joseph son of David, do not be afraid to take Mary home as your wife, because what is conceived in her is from the Holy Spirit. She will give birth to a son, and you are to give him the name Jesus, because he will save his people from their sins." (Matthew 1:20–21)

the story of Jesus' life, they have some differences and each book emphasises different things about Jesus' life. So, it is important to read all four books in order to get an idea of Jesus' life.

► This painting on the wall of a church shows the three wise men visiting Mary and the baby Jesus.

Weblink: www.CurriculumVisions.com

Epistles (letters)

The first followers of Jesus established many Christian communities. They sent these communities letters instructing the members about the Christian way of life and telling them how to deal with local problems.

Many of these letters were written by a man named Paul, an early Christian **MISSIONARY** who founded many new churches.

The letters of Paul and other early Christian leaders are all gathered together in 21 books. Together, these books are called Epistles (or letters). The books of letters make up almost one-third of the New Testament.

Acts

The Book of Acts is the first written history of the Christian church. Most of the book describes the organisation of the church and events that happened in the years after the death of Jesus.

Acts 2: The Holy Spirit and the Day of Pentecost

When the day of Pentecost came, they were all together in one place... They saw what seemed to be tongues of fire that separated and came to rest on each of them. All of them were filled with the Holy Spirit and began to speak in other tongues as the Spirit enabled them.
(Acts 2:1–4)

Some of the stories in Acts tell of how early Christians faced many obstacles and how some were killed.

Many chapters in this book also describe how Paul worked to spread Christianity and the things that happened to him.

He made no distinction between us and them, for he purified their hearts by faith. (Acts 15:9)

Revelation

The Book of Revelation tells about a time in the future, when God destroys evil for all time. This book describes how, before this happens, a new Messiah will come to Earth to prepare people.

Revelation 7: Life everlasting

After this I looked and there before me was a great multitude that no one could count, from every nation, tribe, people and language, standing before the throne and in front of the Lamb. They were wearing white robes and were holding palm branches in their hands. And they cried out in a loud voice: Salvation belongs to our God, who sits on the throne, and to the Lamb.
(Revelation 7:9–10)

The history of the Bible

It took 1,500 years to create the book that Christians think is the greatest book ever written.

The Bible Mary Jones worked so hard to buy (pages 4 to 5) was written in the Welsh language. It had been translated from English. But the first Bible was not written in English. The story of how the Bible came to be written in English is very interesting.

The book

Imagine getting 40 authors in ten different countries, speaking three different languages, to write a book over a 1,500 year period. This is a bit what it was like to write the Bible. The Bible started some 2,000 years before the birth of Jesus Christ. On a hill in the Middle East called Mt Sinai, God revealed himself to Moses. God then instructed Moses to write the first five books of what would later become the Holy Bible.

Over time, other books were added by other writers. These books were written in Hebrew and Greek and contained hymns, stories, poems, histories, **PROVERBS** and other writings. They were written on scrolls made of dried animal skin, called parchment.

By about 500 BC, Jewish people had gathered these writings together into the 39 books of the Hebrew Bible, which they also called the Miqra ('Scripture') or the Tanakh, and which Christians call the Old Testament.

Soon after this, the land of the Jews became part of the Greek empire and so the next part of the Bible – the historical books called the Apocrypha – were written not in Hebrew, but in Greek. At the same time, around 250 BC in Alexandria, Egypt, the earlier parts of the Hebrew Bible were also translated into Greek.

▶ In the Jewish religion, the first five books of the Bible are called the TORAH. The Torah is handwritten, in Hebrew, onto scrolls by specially-trained scribes. A section of the Torah is read aloud from the scroll each week during worship in the synagogue. An entire Torah scroll, if completely unravelled, is over 50 m long.

When Christianity began, the Christians used these Greek translations as their copies of the Old Testament.

The New Testament books

The first New Testament books were written in the first century after Jesus' death. They were probably written in a language called Aramaic, which was the language Jesus spoke. But there are no copies of these books left for us to see.

The books of the New Testament were written on papyrus, which is a thin, paper-like material made from crushed and flattened stalks of the papyrus reed. Papyrus sheets could not be made into scrolls like the animal skins because they are too brittle, so they were bound into books as flat sheets. People called these groups of sheets a codex.

The oldest copies of the New Testament known to exist today include the Codex Alexandrius and the Codex Sinaiticus (in the British Museum). They were produced in the early 4th century AD, on the instructions of Roman Emperor Constantine.

In AD 382, a monk called Jerome started translating the New Testament from its original Greek into Latin.

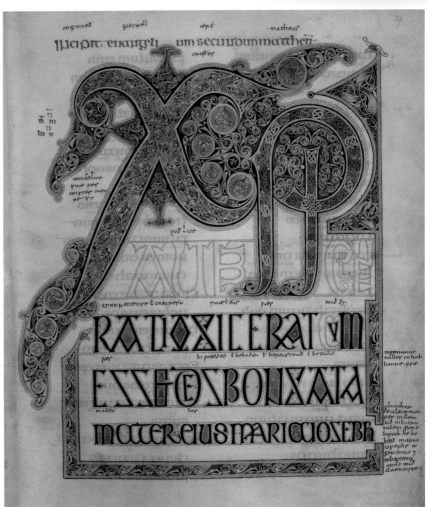

▲ This is a page from the Lindisfarne Gospels, part of the New Testament. They were handwritten in about AD 700, that is just over 1,300 years ago.

Other people then began to translate it into many other languages. But then, on the orders of the Pope, all of these translations were ordered to be destroyed and only the Latin version was allowed. This is because only the priests and monks knew how to read and write Latin and so it helped them to control who could read God's holy word. This was a bid for power that was to last for eight hundred years.

The Bible is translated into English

It was only in the late 1300s that a man named John Wycliffe, an Oxford professor, set about the task of writing out the Bible in English so that everyone could read it. He translated the Bible from the Latin.

In 1450 Johann Gutenberg invented the printing press. His first books were Bibles – printed in Latin. He made 180 of these beautiful illustrated Bibles in colour (see opposite). So although the Bible was still mainly in Latin, it had taken its first step to becoming more widely available.

William Tyndale was the first person ever to print the Bible in the English language. Tyndale was persecuted for this and had to flee from England. Every copy that reached England and that the church could find was burned. Tyndale himself was eventually caught and burned at the stake.

In the meantime, for reasons largely unconnected with the Bible, King Henry VIII of England broke away from the church in Rome. As leader of the new Anglican (English) church, he ordered his archbishop, Thomas Cranmer, to publish the 'Great Bible' in English. It became the

▲ William Tyndale with the first Bible printed in English.

first English Bible authorised for public use, and it was distributed to every church. This Bible, now called the Cranmer Bible, was chained to the pulpit, and a person called a 'reader' was provided so that those who could not read for themselves could hear the word of God in plain English.

After Henry VIII's death, his daughter, Queen Mary, came to the throne. She was a Roman Catholic and so this was a new setback for the Bible in English. Many people fled to Switzerland and there, in Geneva, they began a new translation, now called the Geneva Bible. It was the first Bible to add numbers to the verses, making it easier to reference.

When Queen Elizabeth I gained the throne of England, it was possible to distribute English Bibles again and the Geneva Bible became widely read. This is the Bible whose quotes are found in William Shakespeare's plays.

In 1604, King James commissioned 50 scholars to produce a new version of the Bible translated from Hebrew and Greek versions. This Bible was the one used for the next 250 years until the English Revised Version of 1881–1885.

Since this time there have been many more translations of the Bible into English, each designed to be more easily read.

▼ This is a page from the world's first printed Bible. It is called the Gutenberg Bible and was made in 1450, that is over 550 years ago.

► This boy is reading a children's Bible. This is a version which uses simple words, so it can be understood by young children.

Using the Bible

There are many ways to read and to use the Bible.

Reading the Bible

There are many different ways to read the Bible.

In Christian worship, the Bible may be read as part of the service. In some services, the priest may give a sermon explaining a part of the Bible.

In Jewish worship, a different part of the Torah is read each week during services so that the entire Torah is read every year.

Many people also read the Bible on their own. Some people read it cover-to-cover. Others like to open the Bible to a random page and read whichever book they come to first.

The books of the Bible are not always in chronological order. That is, events in one book may happen before or after events in the next book. Also, some of the books, such as the Gospels, tell the same story (the story of Jesus' life) in different ways.

However you read the stories in the Bible, it is important to think about the meaning of each story.

Learning lessons from the Bible

There are many different lessons in the Bible. Some of these, such as the PARABLES and proverbs, are easy to learn. For example, everyone can easily understand the lesson of this proverb:

> *A gentle answer turns away wrath, but a harsh word stirs up anger.*
> *(Proverbs 15:1)*

However, many of the stories in the Bible are harder to understand and you may need to think about what these stories mean for a long time, or discuss them with other people.

Can you believe in the Bible?

Some people believe that the Bible is the word of God and is accurate down to smallest details.

Other people believe that the Bible is a set of stories which are used to make hard ideas easy. For example, in Genesis it says that God created the Earth in six days. Some people believe this really means six days, and evolution did not happen. Other people believe that six days was simply a nice way of writing 'a long time' or that one of God's days lasted for a billion years. Still others believe that God created the world in six days, but after that He let evolution do the rest.

You can see that there are many different views about the things that happen in the Bible. Which view you take must be something you make up your own mind about.

Using the Bible for song

People have been using the Bible as an inspiration for song since the earliest times.

Parts of the Bible have been sung or chanted since it was first written. Songs are often easier to remember than words in a book, so songs are an easy way of learning the word of God. Songs can also make us feel a certain way, such as joyful or sad.

Psalms were sung, or chanted every day in ancient Jewish worship. Sometimes, the Jewish priests, or rabbis would sing a line and then the congregation would sing the next line. Today, the Bible is still sung or chanted during Jewish worship.

When Christianity began, Christians also used song in their services. At first, Christian congregations sang or chanted the Psalms, but over time new types of music and new songs of praise began to be used.

Gregorian chants

Beginning in the 6th century, monks developed a way of singing without any musical instruments to help them. This music was performed by choirs and was called 'plain chant' or 'Gregorian chant' because Pope Gregory (540–604) first encouraged this type of singing.

By the 14th and 15th centuries additional voices and more complicated ways of singing were introduced.

There are many places in the Old Testament where singing is referred to, such as:

Then Moses and the Israelites sang this song to the LORD:
"Hear this, you kings! Listen, you rulers! I will sing to the LORD, I will sing; with song I will praise the LORD, the God of Israel." (Judges 5:3)

Miriam sang to them:
"Sing to the LORD, for he is highly exalted. The horse and its rider he has hurled into the sea."
(Exodus 15:21)

The New Testament also talks about singing God's praises, for example:

Let the word of Christ dwell in you richly as you teach and admonish one another with all wisdom, and as you sing psalms, hymns and spiritual songs with gratitude in your hearts to God.
(Colossians 3:16)

Speak to one another with psalms, hymns and spiritual songs. Sing and make music in your heart to the Lord. (Ephesians 5:19)

Weblink: www.CurriculumVisions.com

A new time of songs

When the Protestant Church split away from the Roman Catholic Church in the 16th century, the Protestants began to write many new songs praising God, called hymns. These were meant to be sung by the entire congregation, not only the priests or monks.

To begin with, the writers used parts of the Bible **SCRIPTURE**, especially the Psalms, for the words. Later, people used the meaning of the Bible rather than its exact words. New music was also written, to make it easier for people to sing.

Isaac Watts (1674–1748) was one of the first people to write these new kinds of hymns in English. He wrote more than 600 hymns.

This is one of Isaac Watts most famous hymns. It was written for Christmas and is called *Joy to the World*. The music was written by the composer Handel.

Joy to the world, the Lord is come!
Let Earth receive her King;
Let every heart prepare Him room,
And Heaven and nature sing,
And Heaven and nature sing,
And Heaven, and Heaven,
*   and nature sing.*

You can see that this hymn takes its ideas from the Bible even though the words are not from the Bible.

Amazing Grace

Many hymns are based on ideas found in the Bible. The hymn *Amazing Grace* was written by an American, John Newton. Newton was a slave trader who one day realised that slavery was wrong. After this he began preaching and wrote many hymns. The verse, *'I was blind, but now I see'* comes from the New Testament, John 9:25.

Amazing Grace, how sweet the sound
That sav'd a wretch like me!
I once was lost, but now am found,
Was blind, but now I see.

'Twas grace that taught my heart to fear,
And grace my fears reliev'd;
How precious did that grace appear,
The hour I first believ'd!

Thro' many dangers, toils and snares,
I have already come;
'Tis grace has brought me safe thus far,
And grace will lead me home.

The Lord has promis'd good to me,
His word my hope secures;
He will my shield and
*   portion be,*
As long as life endures.

Yes, when this flesh and
*   heart shall fail,*
And mortal life shall
*   cease;*
I shall possess, within
*   the veil,*
A life of joy and peace.

The Earth shall soon
*   dissolve like snow,*
The Sun forbear to shine;
But God, who call'd me
*   here below,*
Will be forever mine.

The Ten Commandments

God gave Moses the Ten Commandments. These are the basic laws that we should all live by.

The Bible is a guidebook to life. The Bible sets out the rules that we should live by if we are to be at peace with God, people and all living things.

After God had delivered the Jewish people out of slavery in Egypt, he gave Moses laws by which they should live. The most important of these laws are called the Ten Commandments. You can find them in the Old Testament Book of Exodus, Chapter 20.

If you look at the commandments opposite carefully, you will see that, although they were written 3,400 years ago, they are still as important today as they ever were. There are many other guidelines and rules in the Bible, but many people feel that the Ten Commandments are the most important.

▼ The first words of each of the Ten Commandments in Hebrew.

Weblink: www.CurriculumVisions.com

Exodus 20:1–17

And God spoke all these words:

"I am the LORD your God, who brought you out of Egypt, out of the land of slavery.

"You shall have no other gods before me.

"You shall not make for yourself an idol in the form of anything in Heaven above or on the Earth beneath or in the waters below. You shall not bow down to them or worship them...

"You shall not misuse the name of the LORD your God, for the LORD will not hold anyone guiltless who misuses his name.

"Remember the Sabbath day by keeping it holy.

Six days you shall labour and do all your work, but the seventh day is a Sabbath to the LORD your God. On it you shall not do any work... For in six days the LORD made the Heavens and the Earth, the sea, and all that is in them, but he rested on the seventh day. Therefore the LORD blessed the Sabbath day and made it holy.

"Honour your father and your mother, so that you may live long in the land the LORD your God is giving you.

"You shall not murder.

"You shall not commit adultery.

"You shall not steal.

"You shall not give false testimony against your neighbour.

"You shall not covet your neighbour's house. You shall not covet your neighbour's wife, or his manservant or maidservant, his ox or donkey, or anything that belongs to your neighbour."

Poetry in the Bible

The Bible was written so that it would be a pleasure to read as well as being the book of life.

When you read a book, you notice if it is interesting. But did you realise that part of what you enjoy is the way the story or the information is written, not just what it tells you? Some books are written in very beautiful language.

The Bible is easy and enjoyable to read because much of it is written as a form of poetry.

The Song of Songs

Some of the Bible is written in poetry. For example, the Song of Songs is a book in the Old Testament. It is a long poem about God's love. Here is a part of it:

I am a rose of Sharon,
*   a lily of the valleys.*
Like a lily among thorns
*   is my darling among the maidens.*
Like an apple tree among the trees
*   of the forest*
*   is my beloved among the young men.*
*   I delight to sit in his shade,*
*   and his fruit is sweet to my taste.*
He has taken me to the banquet hall,
*   and his banner over me is love.*
Strengthen me with raisins,
*   refresh me with apples,*
*   for I am faint with love.*
His left arm is under my head,
*   and his right arm embraces me.*

Poetry can be lost in translation

One reason why some people like to read a work in its original language is that it may lose something in translation. Many people feel this way and try to read their religious texts in the original language.

Take a look at this. It comes from the Old Testament book of the prophet Nahum.

First the English translation:

She (Ninevah) is empty,
desolate, and waste!
(Nahum 2:10)

These are the Hebrew words it is translated from:

Ninevah Bukah, Mebukah,
Mebullakah!

You many not be able to read the Hebrew, but you can see that it contains similar words repeated one after another – a kind of poetry which makes the passage more enjoyable to read.

So when people translate the Bible they have the task of trying to keep the poetry or deciding not to bother at all.

Weblink: www.CurriculumVisions.com

The Beatitudes

Here is one of the most famous examples of poetry in the New Testament. It is called the Beatitudes. Beatitude means blessing.

God gave Moses the Ten Commandments on Mount Sinai (Exodus 20). Instead of repeating, "You shall not...," Jesus summed up God's teaching in blessings. Notice how much more powerful it is because it is said in such a beautiful way.

▲ Some of the poetry in the Old Testament describes a garden and vineyards like the ones in this stained glass window from a modern synagogue.

The Beatitudes from the Sermon on the Mount

Now when he saw the crowds, he went up on a mountainside and sat down. His disciples came to him, and he began to teach them saying:

"Blessed are the poor in spirit,
for theirs is the kingdom of Heaven.

Blessed are those who mourn,
for they will be comforted.

Blessed are the meek,
for they will inherit the Earth.

Blessed are those who hunger and thirst for righteousness,
for they will be filled.

Blessed are the merciful,
for they will be shown mercy.

Blessed are the pure in heart,
for they will see God.

Blessed are the peacemakers,
for they will be called sons of God.

Blessed are those who are persecuted because of righteousness,
for theirs is the kingdom of Heaven.

Blessed are you when people insult you, persecute you and falsely say all kinds of evil against you because of me. Rejoice and be glad, because great is your reward in Heaven, for in the same way they persecuted the prophets who were before you."

(Matthew 5:1–12)

Parables in the Bible

A parable is a word picture used to help people understand the difficult ideas in the Bible.

Many of the stories in the Bible were written in order to help people remember important ideas.

A **PARABLE** is a story with a lesson or a moral. By listening to or reading these stories, we can easily see how the meaning of the story is important to us.

Jewish religious leaders had used parables since early times and the Old Testament is full of these stories.

Jesus, who was, of course, a Jewish teacher, also used parables to teach. In fact, parables were the most common way that Jesus got His message across. Over a third of the Gospels of Matthew, Mark and Luke contain parables told by Jesus.

Like a skilful artist, Jesus painted pictures with short and simple words, telling stories that often had surprising endings and so were fun to listen to as well.

Jesus' parables often compare the common with the unusual. For example, in the parable of the sower and the seeds of grain (*Luke 8:4–15; Mark 4:3–9; Matthew 13:3–9*), Jesus compared the seeds of grain to the people of the world.

A farmer went out to sow his seed. As he was scattering the seed, some fell along the path; it was trampled on, and the birds of the air ate it up.

Some fell on rock, and when it came up, the plants withered because they had no moisture.

Other seed fell among thorns, which grew up with it and choked the plants.

Still other seed fell on good soil. It came up and yielded a crop, a hundred times more than was sown…

This is the meaning of the parable: The seed is the word of God. Those along the path are the ones who hear, and then the devil comes and takes away the word from their hearts, so that they may not believe and be saved.

Those on the rock are the ones who receive the word with joy when they hear it, but they have no root. They believe for a while, but in the time of testing they fall away.

The seed that fell among thorns stands for those who hear, but as they go on their way they are choked by life's worries, riches and pleasures, and they do not mature.

But the seed on good soil stands for those with a noble and good heart, who hear the word, retain it, and by persevering produce a crop.

(Luke 8:4–15)

▲ Here is Luke's version of the sower and seed parable.

Weblink: www.CurriculumVisions.com

Why did Jesus use this parable? His audience was mostly farmers, so they could easily understand the idea of some seed taking root and the rest failing.

But Jesus is telling people as well that just listening to the word of God is not enough. You have to believe it and act on it, or you will not be useful to God, but be like the seed that fell on the path, or on the rock, or among the thorns.

▲ Singing Psalms in church.

Psalms in the Bible

A Psalm is a poem or song with a religious meaning. One whole book of the Old Testament contains nothing but Psalms.

The Book of Psalms is the longest book in the Bible. It is also unusual because it contains only poems. The Hebrew word for this book is *Sepher Tehillim*, which means 'Book of Praises' and all of the poems are in praise of God. (The Greek translation is *Psalmoi*, and from this we get the English word Psalm.)

There are 150 Psalms in the book, written by many authors, including Moses, King David and King Solomon.

The Psalms were meant to be sung or chanted during worship and may have been accompanied by music.

Each Psalm is a prayer to the Lord arranged in beautiful words. All Psalms have been set to music through the ages, and are still being set to modern music today. For example, Psalm 137, *"The mourning of the exiles in Babylon,"* has been made into traditional hymns, spiritual (African-American) hymns, reggae (Afro-Caribbean) songs and modern pop songs. Part of it goes *"By the rivers of Babylon, there we sat down, yea, we wept, when we remembered Zion."*

The most widely known of the Psalms is Psalm 23, *"The Lord is my shepherd, I shall not want"*. This Psalm is sung or spoken by Christians all over the world.

Psalm 51, *"Have mercy on me O God,"* is also known as the miserere (pronounced mis-er-rare-uh) and is one of the most widely sung Psalms in **ORTHODOX** churches.

Here are passages from some of the most famous Psalms:

Weblink: www.CurriculumVisions.com

Psalm 23:1–6

The LORD is my shepherd,
   I shall not be in want.
He makes me lie down in green
   pastures,
he leads me beside quiet waters,
he restores my soul.
He guides me in paths of righteousness
   for his name's sake.

Even though I walk
through the valley of the shadow
   of death,
I will fear no evil,
for you are with me;
your rod and your staff,
they comfort me.

You prepare a table before me
in the presence of my enemies.
You anoint my head with oil;
my cup overflows.

Surely goodness and love will follow
me all the days of my life,
and I will dwell in the house of
   the LORD forever.

Psalm 51: 1–3

Have mercy on me, O God,
according to your unfailing love;
according to your great compassion
blot out my transgressions.

Wash away all my iniquity
and cleanse me from my sin.

For I know my transgressions,
and my sin is always before me.

Psalm 103:1–9

Praise the LORD, O my soul;
all my inmost being, praise his
holy name.

Praise the LORD, O my soul,
and forget not all his benefits –

who forgives all your sins
and heals all your diseases,

who redeems your life from the pit
and crowns you with love and
   compassion,

who satisfies your desires with good
   things
so that your youth is renewed like
   the eagle's.

The LORD works righteousness
and justice for all the oppressed.

He made known his ways
   to Moses,
his deeds to the people
   of Israel:

The LORD is
compassionate and
   gracious,
slow to anger,
abounding in love.

He will not always
   accuse,
nor will he
harbour
his anger
forever.

Letters in the Bible

When the Christian church began, the first Christian communities had no books to guide them. So the leaders of the church wrote letters of guidance.

After the death of Jesus, the **DISCIPLES** and other followers of Jesus began to preach and convert people to Christianity and set up Christian communities.

Because Jesus did not write anything down, these people did not have any writings to guide them or to give to the new Christian communities. These communities had many questions about their new faith and needed guidance. So, the early leaders wrote many letters to these communities to help them.

What is in the letters?

The letters written by Christian leaders and included in the Bible explain Jesus' message, and also how to organise their communities and how to conduct worship services.

Most of the letters were written by Paul, who converted to Christianity after Jesus' death and founded many churches. Almost one-third of the New Testament is made up of Paul's letters (which are also called Epistles).

The early Christians were living in difficult times. They were hunted down and often put to death for their faith, so they needed to be told over and over again what it was that they had to believe, just as we do today.

Here is a part of the letter to the Hebrew Christians *(Hebrews 13:1–6)*:

Keep on loving each other as brothers.

Do not forget to entertain strangers, for by so doing some people have entertained angels without knowing it.

Remember those in prison as if you were their fellow prisoners, and those who are mistreated as if you yourselves were suffering.

Marriage should be honoured by all, and the marriage bed kept pure, for God will judge the adulterer and all the sexually immoral. Keep your lives free from the love of money and be content with what you have, because God has said,
"Never will I leave you; never will I forsake you."

So we say with confidence,
"The Lord is my helper; I will not be afraid. What can man do to me?"

The writer is telling Christians they can use the Hebrew scriptures, and quoting from Deuteronomy 31 and Psalm 118.

Weblink: www.CurriculumVisions.com

◀▼These paintings in a church show some of the early Christians who died for their beliefs. *(Left)* Saint Andrew is shown with an x-shaped cross like the one he was crucified on.

Index

Abraham 10
Acts 6, 12–13
Adam and Eve 10
Amazing Grace 21
Anglican 16
Apocrypha 2, 7, 14
apostle 2, 6
Aramaic 15

Babylon 7, 28
Beatitudes 25

church 2, 6, 13, 16, 21, 28, 30, 31
commandment 2, 6, 10, 22–23, 25

Deuteronomy 11, 30
disciple 2, 30

Egypt 10, 11, 14, 22
Epistle 2, 6, 9, 12–13, 30
Exodus 10, 11, 20, 22–23

Garden of Eden 6
Genesis 6, 9, 10, 19
Gospel 2, 6, 12, 15, 19, 26
Greek 7, 14, 15, 28
Gregorian chant 20

Hebrew 2, 6, 7, 14, 22, 24, 28, 30
hymns 11, 14, 21, 28

Isaac Watts 21
Israel 2, 7, 10, 11

Jesus Christ 2, 6, 8, 11, 12–13, 14, 15, 19, 25, 26–27, 30
Jewish 6, 7, 10, 11, 14, 19, 20, 22, 26
John 12, 21

King James Bible 7, 16

Latin 7, 15–16
Leviticus 11
Luke 12, 26

Mark 12, 26
Mary Jones 4–5, 14
Matthew 12, 25, 26
Messiah 2, 11, 13
miserere 28
missionary 2, 13
Moses 6, 10, 11, 14, 22, 25, 28

Nahum 24
New Testament 2, 6, 12–13, 15, 20, 21, 25, 30
Numbers 11

Old Testament 2, 6, 10–11, 14, 15, 20, 22, 24, 25, 26, 28
Orthodox 2, 7, 28

papyrus 15
parable 2, 19, 26–27
Paul 13, 30
Promised Land 2, 11
prophet 2, 8, 9, 11, 24
Protestant 2, 7, 8, 21
Proverbs 2, 11, 14, 19
Psalms 7, 11, 20, 21, 28–29, 30

reggae 28
repent/repentance 2, 11
resurrection 2, 8, 12
Revelation 6, 12, 13
Roman Catholic 2, 7, 16, 21

sacrifice 2, 11
scripture 2, 7, 14, 21, 30
Sermon on the Mount 25
Solomon 9, 11, 28
song 11, 20–21, 28
Song of Songs/Song of Solomon 11, 24

Tanakh 14
Ten Commandments 6, 10, 22–23, 25, 30
Torah 2, 14, 19

Curriculum Visions

Curriculum Visions is a registered trademark of Atlantic Europe Publishing Company Ltd.

Atlantic Europe Publishing

Dedicated Web Site
There's more about other great Curriculum Visions packs and a wealth of supporting information available at our dedicated web site:

www.CurriculumVisions.com

First published in 2005 by
Atlantic Europe Publishing Company Ltd
Copyright © 2005
Atlantic Europe Publishing Company Ltd

All rights reserved. No part of this publication may be reproduced, stored in a retrieval system, or transmitted in any form or by any means, electronic, mechanical, photocopying, recording or otherwise, without prior permission of the Publisher.

Authors
Brian Knapp, BSc, PhD, and Lisa Magloff, MA
Religious Advisers
Reverend Colin Bass, BSc, MA, and Aella Gage
Art Director
Duncan McCrae, BSc
Senior Designer
Adele Humphries, BA
Acknowledgements
The publishers would like to thank the following for their help and advice:
St James Church, Muswell Hill, London;
St John the Baptist Church, Wightman Road, London; Father George Christidis of St Nictarios, Battersea, London; Rector Father Terence Phipps of St James Church, Spanish Place, London; Kezia Humphries.

Scripture throughout this book is taken from the HOLY BIBLE, NEW INTERNATIONAL VERSION®. Copyright © 1973, 1978, 1984 International Bible Society. Used by permission of Zondervan. All rights reserved.

Photographs
The Earthscape Editions photolibrary, except pages 4 and 5 Kyle Wood, 10 ShutterStock, 15 *British Library*, 16 and 17 *The Granger Collection, New York.*

Illustrations
David Woodroffe

Designed and produced by
Earthscape Editions

Printed in China by
WKT Company Ltd

The story of the Bible
– Curriculum Visions
A CIP record for this book is available from the British Library

Paperback ISBN 1 86214 483 4
Hardback ISBN 1 86214 484 2

This product is manufactured from sustainable managed forests. For every tree cut down at least one more is planted.